W9-BGG-388

WORMS

Jen Green

Grolier
an imprint of

SCHOLASTIC

www.scholastic.com/librarypublishing

Published 2009 by Grolier
An Imprint of Scholastic Library Publishing
Old Sherman Turnpike
Danbury, Connecticut 06816

For The Brown Reference Group
Project Editor: Jolyon Goddard
Picture Researchers: Clare Newman,
Sophie Mortimer
Designer: Sarah Williams
Managing Editor: Tim Harris

Volume ISBN-13: 978-0-7172-8078-0
Volume ISBN-10: 0-7172-8078-0

Library of Congress
Cataloging-in-Publication Data

Nature's children. Set 6.
   p. cm.
  Includes index.
  ISBN-13: 978-0-7172-8085-8
  ISBN-10: 0-7172-8085-3
  1. Animals--Encyclopedias, Juvenile. I.
Grolier (Firm)
  QL49.N387 2009
  590.3--dc22
                        2008014675

Printed and bound in China

PICTURE CREDITS

Front Cover: Shutterstock: Pakhnyushcha.

Back Cover: Shutterstock: John A.
Anderson, Mircea Bezergheanu, Stephan
Kerkhofs, Mashe.

Corbis: Sally A. Morgan 6, Robert Pickett 22,
26, Robert Yin 9; NHPA: G. I. Bernard 30,
Laurie Campbell 13, Stephen Dalton 17,
36–37, 38, 41, 45, Ralph and Daphne Keller
14, Eric Soder 29; Shutterstock: David
Anderson 5, Clearviewstock 18, 33, ENOXH
2-3, Joan Ramon Mendo Escoda 4, Kelpfish
10, Olga Kolos 25, n4photovideo 42,
Pakhnyushcha 21, 46.

Contents

Fact File: Worms 4

Mysterious Creatures 7

Thousands of Worms 8

Habitats 11

Body Shape 12

Earthworms 15

Long and Thin 16

Getting Around 19

Eating Soil 20

Safe Burrows 23

Lugworms 24

Going Underground 27

Active at Night 28

Finding Food 31

Helpful Worms 32

Worm Pests 34

Survivors 35

Feature Photo 36–37

Worm Senses 39

Danger Everywhere 40

Feathered Foes 43

Bloodsuckers 44

Mating Time. 47

In the Water 48

Words to Know 49

Find Out More 51

Index. 52

FACT FILE: Worms

Phyla	Segmented worms (Annelida), flatworms (Platyhelminthes), and roundworms (Nematoda)
Classes	Various, including earthworms and leaches (Clitellata), marine worms (Polychaeta), and tapeworms (Cestoda)
Families	Hundreds of families
Genera	Thousands of genera
Species	Many thousands, including at least 9,000 species of segmented worms
World distribution	Everywhere except where the earth is permanently frozen or extremely dry
Habitat	On land, mainly underground; seas and oceans, seashores, freshwater ponds, and streams; some live inside other animals
Distinctive physical characteristics	Long, thin body with a distinct head and tail; body often divided into segments that move semi-independently
Habits	Vary with type—earthworms mostly live underground, burrowing through soil
Diet	Varies with type—earthworms eat soil and plant and animal remains; marine worms catch and eat food floating in the sea

Introduction

The most familiar kind of worm to most people
is the earthworm. This long, wriggly animal is
most often seen coming out of the soil when it
rains. However, there is a staggering variety of
different types of worms. Many worms, including
earthworms, leeches, lugworms, and tube worms,
belong to a group of animals called **annelids**
(AH-NUH-LIDS). Flatworms and roundworms are
other large groups of worms. These groups
include many free-living worms. But they also
include tapeworms and hookworms, which live
as adults inside other animals, including humans!

**Earthworms are also
known as night crawlers.**

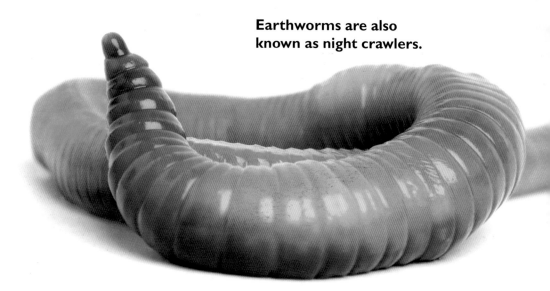

Earthworms help make land fertile by spreading nutrients through the soil.

Mysterious Creatures

Which mysterious creature can feel without hands and move without legs? Which animal has no eyes, yet can "see" light and dark? Which animal is neither male nor female? The answer to all these riddles is: a worm.

Worms are surprising animals. They are strong and tough in some ways. Some kinds of worms can survive if they are cut in two.

Of all the creatures in the animal kingdom, the little worm is one of our greatest friends. Worms help the soil stay rich and fertile, so crops can flourish in the fields and flowers can bloom in gardens. However, some kinds of worms are not so friendly—in fact, they are deadly! Worms are varied creatures.

Thousands of Worms

A worm is a long, thin, soft animal without bones
or legs. Would you be surprised to learn that
there are more than 20,000 different **species**,
or kinds, of worms in the world? Earthworms
are the best-known family of worms, but there
are other families, too, including the leaf-shaped
flatworms and the long, threadlike roundworms.

Most people call any long, thin creature they
see a worm. Yet many wormlike animals are
not really worms at all. Caterpillars and grubs
are legless creatures with a long body, but they
are insects, not worms. Some animals are even
called worms but are not! Silkworms are young
silk-moth caterpillars, glowworms are really
beetles, and slowworms are a family of lizards
with no legs.

A black-and-white flatworm swims over green corals in the Pacific Ocean near the Philippines.

A spiral-gilled tube worm looks more like a plant than an animal. This worm lives in brain coral.

Habitats

Where would you expect to find worms? In the ground? Worms can be found in a lot of other places, too. Worms like water and damp places. Many worms live in the sea, both on the seashore and in deep water. However, not all worms that live in water like salty seawater. Some worms live in freshwater ponds and streams.

On land, worms are found almost all over the world. Two places that you will not find worms are the polar regions, where the land is always frozen, and deserts, where the ground is too dry. Some worms live inside other animals. Wherever you live, earthworms are likely to be there, too, in the soil under your feet.

Body Shape

Worms come in different shapes and colors. Earthworms are long, pink, and wriggly. In the sea, there is a worm called a sea mouse that has a short, brown body covered with shiny hair. It looks just like a mouse. Bristleworms also live in the sea. Some have a bright orange body covered with sharp spines. Unlike earthworms, they have eyes and **tentacles**, which they use to catch their food. Ragworms have flaps that look like torn strips of rag along the sides of their body.

Worms come in different sizes, too. Vinegar worms, which live in vinegar, are so small you can only see them with a microscope. The largest worms are tapeworms, which live inside the body of other animals. They can grow up to 40 feet (12 m) long.

To a passing predator the squat body of a sea mouse looks like a small rock covered in seaweed.

The tail of a giant
Australian earthworm
pokes out of the ground.

Earthworms

The little earthworm you see wriggling through the grass is a member of a large family. There are an amazing 3,000 species of earthworms. They are found all over the world and in very large numbers. There are about two billion earthworms living in 1 square mile (2.5 sq km) of grassland.

The average earthworm is about 8 inches (20 cm) long. Some of its cousins, however, can be much larger or smaller. The smallest earthworms are no longer than your fingernail. But the giant Australian earthworm is more than 10 feet (3 m) long—as long as a small car. The largest earthworm, the giant African worm, is in a league of its own. When fully grown, this worm measures 22 feet (7 m) long.

Long and Thin

Worms are known for their long, skinny body. Some worms are smooth and rounded, while others are ridged and bumpy. An earthworm's body is divided into thin, ring-shaped **segments**. Each segment can move separately from the others, which helps the worm slide along.

The rear end is the tail, and the front end contains the worm's mouth and simple brain. Can you tell which end is which? If you look closely at an earthworm, you will see that the tail end is flatter and more blunted, and the front is pointy.

Take another look at the worm. Can you see a smooth ring circling the creature's body? This ring is called the **saddle**, and only adult earthworms have one.

Common earthworms, like this one, have about 180 body segments. The longest worms may have 600!

Earthworms have a smooth, sleek body. That allows them to move easily through soil.

Getting Around

Earthworms have no legs, so how do they move around? That is where the segments of the worm's body come in handy. They make the worm's body stretchy and able to change shape. Different parts of the body can be stretched out so they are long and thin or squashed up to be short and fat.

The worm's skin looks smooth and slimy, but on the underside of each segment there are four pairs of tiny **bristles**. The bristles help the worm grip the soil. When tunneling underground, the worm moves through the soil by making the tail section of its body short and fat, so it fills the tunnel. Bristles anchor the tail, while the worm makes its front end thin and wriggles through cracks in the soil. Then it swells its front end, makes its tail thin, and pulls the rear part of its body forward though the tunnel.

Eating Soil

When the ground is very hard and dry, a worm cannot tunnel by forcing its body into cracks. Instead, it eats its way through the ground, swallowing the soil! A few mouthfuls of earth would not make a tasty meal for a human. To the worm, however, soil is a complete meal and contains many things that are good to eat. The soil passes along the worm's **intestines**, which run right down its body. The good things are digested, and the remains pass out at the tail. The worm's droppings are called a **worm cast**. They look just like a coiled-up worm. Some worms leave their casts underground, but many leave them on the surface. If you see worm casts on your lawn or in a grassy field, you will know that worms live there!

A worm will eat the
remains of plants and
animals as well as soil.

Going underground—
an earthworm
carefully enters
its burrow.

Safe Burrows

Some kinds of earthworms live on the surface, under a log or a pile of leaves. However, most live underground in **burrows**. Some worms make their burrows just below the surface. Others prefer to live 3 to 4 feet (90 to 120 cm) underground.

To make its burrow, a worm digs a series of little connecting tunnels. Several passages lead up to the surface. Deep in the earth, there may be a little round chamber for sleeping. As it wriggles down its hole, a worm may block the entrance with leaves and twigs. This cover hides the burrow so other animals cannot find it. It also keeps the worm's home moist in dry weather and warm when it is cold outside.

Lugworms

Have you seen worm casts on the seashore?
These little piles of sand and mud are made not
by earthworms but by their distant cousins called
lugworms. Beneath the sand the lugworm lives
in a little U-shaped burrow. It swallows the sand
and mud that trickles down into its **lair**. The
worm digests the good things in the mud. Then,
at regular intervals—every 40 minutes or so—it
squirts the waste out of its burrow, like
toothpaste from a tube!

Human fishers use lugworms as **bait** to
catch fish. They dig in the sand for lugworms
wherever they see the casts. To catch lugworms,
however, a fisher must be quick, because they
are very good at burrowing. In a few seconds
they can dig deep into the sand, out of reach
of the fisher's spade.

This is the cast of a lugworm. Lugworms spend most of their life in water. They breathe using feathery gills that run along the sides of their body.

You are more likely to see worms in the grass after it has rained.

Going Underground

If you dig in the ground in summer, especially after it has rained, you will probably unearth a lot of worms. If you dug the same patch in frosty winter weather, you might not find any. So where have the worms gone?

The worms have gone deep underground, where the earth is slightly warmer. In very cold weather, the worm hides in a little chamber at the bottom of its burrow. It curls its body into a tight knot, which stops it from losing body heat. In very dry summer weather, it goes back to this little chamber and curls up in the same way to prevent its body from drying out.

Active at Night

The human body works to a rhythm that lasts
24 hours—one day. In daylight most humans
are awake and active. At night they need rest,
so they lie down and sleep.

A worm's daily cycle also lasts 24 hours, but
it is active at the opposite time you are. During
daylight hours, it rests in its burrow. At night it
comes out to feed. Creatures that are active at
night are called **nocturnal**.

This daily rhythm helps the worm hide from
many animals that spend the hours of daylight
looking for food. A worm would keep to the
same rhythm even if it was moved to a place
that was kept light or dark all the time.

Worm casts on the forest floor are all the evidence you are likely to see of earthworms during the day.

A giant forest-floor flatworm catches a snail among the lush undergrowth of a rain forest in Venezuela.

Finding Food

Earthworms do not eat only soil. They feed on the remains of plants and animals, too. At night, worms come out of their burrows to search for food aboveground. If a worm comes across a prize such as a tasty leaf, it drags it down into its burrow. Later, when the leaf has rotted, the worm can munch through it in the safety of its home.

Many worms that live in water have tentacles on their head to help them catch their food. Some bristleworms have a crown of tentacles that they spread out in the water like a fan. Drifting scraps of food are trapped in the tentacles and become the worm's supper. Other bristleworms are fierce hunters. They comb the ocean bottom for small creatures that they kill for food.

Helpful Worms

You may be surprised to learn that earthworms are very important creatures. Without them, the soil would not be as healthy, and plants would not grow so well. As worms burrow through the soil, they act like little plows, turning the soil over and mixing up the layers. Worm tunnels let air down into the ground, so that plants and animals in the soil can breathe. The burrows let rain in as well, helping water drain through the soil and reach the roots of thirsty plants and trees.

Even worm droppings help keep soil healthy! Worm casts act as a natural fertilizer, providing nourishment that helps plants grow. Farmers and gardeners everywhere owe a big "Thank you!" to the friendly worm.

Earthworms churn up the soil. Their actions benefit plants and other animals, allowing them to breathe underground.

Worm Pests

Earthworms are our friends. But other kinds of worms are not so friendly. Instead, they can do a lot of harm or bring disease. Thin, threadlike roundworms munch through farmers' crops and ruin harvests. In **tropical** countries, types of roundworms called hookworms live in the intestines of their **host**. They bring sickness, and even death, to millions of people and animals.

Tapeworms are long flatworms shaped like ribbons. Like hookworms, tapeworms live inside the intestines of animals, such as dogs, pigs, and cats, and people. The tapeworm sticks to the lining of an animal's intestines with the help of powerful **suckers**, and sometimes also hooks, on its head. It steals the **host** animal's food, so the animal is always thin and hungry. The tapeworm produces thousands of eggs a day. When these pass out in the animal's droppings, they can spread to other creatures, too.

Survivors

In many ways, worms are weak and helpless creatures. But they do have an amazing skill that helps them survive in a dangerous world. If the tail or even the head of an earthworm is cut off by a gardener's spade or bitten off by a **predator**, such as a bird or a mole, the worm is able to mend its body. Slowly it regrows another head or tail.

In warm parts of the world, some sorts of flatworms are even more skilled at survival. If the flatworm is cut in two, both halves live on. In time, each half grows a new head or tail, and the result is two strong, healthy worms.

An earthworm leaves a
worm cast on wet grass
and heads underground.

This hungry toad has used its long tongue to catch a worm.

Worm Senses

Some kinds of worms have eyes. But earthworms have no eyes, ears, or nose. So how do they find their food and escape from predators? The answer lies in the worm's skin, which is extremely sensitive.

On damp, warm nights, earthworms are aboveground, feeling their way through the grass and feeding. But if you shine a light on them, they vanish down their burrows. How does the worm see the light without eyes? Cells in its skin are light-sensitive. So the worm can "feel" light shining on it.

If you stamp your foot, the worm will also vanish. Without ears, a worm cannot hear sounds as we do. But its skin can pick up the vibrations that sounds make. If those tiny waves of sound spell danger, the worm will bolt for home again.

Danger Everywhere

Worms have enemies all around them. All kinds of different animals like to eat soft, juicy worms as their favorite food. In the ocean, fish and other creatures **prey on** worms. On the seashore, gulls search the mud for a tasty snack. In ponds and rivers, frogs and toads catch worms and carefully scrape off the mud before they gulp down their meal.

On dry land, earthworms also have many enemies. Badgers, shrews, and hedgehogs **root** in the soil and suck worms up like spaghetti, with a slurping noise! Did you know that even small creatures such as beetles, centipedes, and slugs catch and eat worms? Even underground in its burrow, no worm is safe. Danger lurks there in the shape of the mole, which tunnels through the soil with its strong claws.

Like worms, moles—their deadly
enemies—live underground.
Moles use their strong claws to
move the earth out of the way.

41

Earthworms can pick up the vibrations made by a robin as the bird hops around looking for food. But not all of them are fast enough to hide in time!

Feathered Foes

Some of the earthworms' deadliest enemies lurk in the air. Garden birds such as blackbirds and robins like nothing better than a juicy worm to eat. Many birds feed their whole families on worms. When the baby birds are growing, they are always hungry! The parent birds catch hundreds of worms and bring them to the nest.

Worms have no weapons such as teeth and claws to fight their feathered foes. But there is one way that even a worm can fight. If a worm is halfway down its burrow when a bird strikes, it uses its bristles to jam its body tightly in the hole. If you've ever seen a blackbird tugging and pulling at an earthworm in the ground, you'll know that the worm does not give up without a fight!

Bloodsuckers

Leeches are close relatives of earthworms. But they live and feed in a very different way. Leeches live in ponds, streams, and damp places. They loop their body into a wave shape to swim along.

Like earthworms, leeches have a body that is divided into segments. But unlike its relative, the leech has suckers on its head and tail. The suckers are used to feed—on other animals' blood! The leech clings on with its suckers to the hide of a large animal such as a cow. The leech bites through the creature's skin and sucks its flesh until the leech's little body fills with blood.

Long ago, doctors often used leeches to draw blood from their patients, because they thought blood-letting would make sick people better. In recent years, the use of medicinal leeches has been making a comeback to treat various disorders.

Leeches like to live in
shallow, almost stagnant
water, so this pond
provides ideal conditions.

When they mate, earthworms are joined together by a coating of sticky mucus as well as by their bristles.

Mating Time

Earthworms are neither male nor female—they are both! That means that each worm can make both eggs and **sperm**, which **fertilizes** eggs. To produce young, however, every worm must still **mate** with another worm, so that the eggs of each are fertilized by the other.

Worms mate at night or early in the morning, particularly when it has been raining. They lie head to tail in the grass or in a burrow, and hook bristles so their bodies join. Later, both worms lay fertilized eggs in the ground. Up to 20 eggs are sealed in a tiny package called a **cocoon**, the size of a grain of wheat. A few months later, baby worms **hatch** from the eggs. When another year has passed, these little worms will be full grown.

In the Water

Worms that live in water mate and have young in ways different from earthworms.

In ponds and streams, leeches make good mothers. Instead of burying their cocoons of eggs, they carry them around in the water. A special pouch under the leech's body keeps the eggs safe until they are ready to hatch.

Sea worms such as bristleworms produce many thousands of eggs, not just a few, like earthworms do. Instead of burying them, they simply scatter them in the water. Most of the eggs do not survive—they are eaten by fish and other creatures. The few that live hatch into strange creatures called **larvae**—young animals that are not yet worms. The tiny larvae swim in the ocean and drift with the sea currents. They feed and gradually grow bigger. In a few months, they become adult worms.

Words to Know

Annelids   A large group of animals that makes up the true worms.

Bait   A piece of food on a hook used to attract and catch fish.

Bristles   Short, stiff hairs.

Burrows   Holes or tunnels in the ground, where animals live.

Cocoon   The tough case that protects the eggs of earthworms and leeches.

Fertilizes   When eggs and sperm combine so that the eggs can develop into young.

Hatch   To break out of an egg.

Host   An animal that has other animals, such as tapeworms, living inside its body and living off its tissues.

Intestines   The long tube in the body in which food is digested.

Lair   A place where a wild animal rests.

Larvae   Early stages in the life of worms.

Mate   To come together to produce young.

Molts	Sheds old feathers to replace them with new ones.
Nestlings	Baby birds that still live in the nest and cannot yet fly.
Perch	A resting place for a bird.
Plumage	A bird's feathers.
Preening	Cleaning and combing the feathers.
Roost	To find a place to sleep at night; a place in which a bird sleeps.
Saliva	A fluid produced in an animal's mouth that helps digest food.
Songbirds	The largest group of birds, to which the crow family belongs.
Species	The scientific word for animals of the same kind that breed together.
Streamlined	Describes a smooth, sleek shape that moves through air or water easily.
Territory	The area in which an animal or group of animals lives and often defends from other animals.

Find Out More

Books

Blaxland, B. *Earthworms, Leeches, and Sea Worms: Annelids*. Invertebrates. New York: Chelsea House Publications, 2002.

Murray, P. *Worms*. Science Around Us. Mankato, Minnesota: Child's World, 2004.

Web sites

Common Earthworm
animals.nationalgeographic.com/animals/invertebrates/ earthworm.html
A profile of the night crawler.

Earthworms
www.zoomschool.com/subjects/invertebrates/earthworm/ Earthwormcoloring.shtml
A diagram and facts about earthworms.

Index

A, B, C

annelids 5

babies 47, 48

brain 16

bristles 19, 46, 47

bristleworms 9, 31, 48

burrows 22, 23, 24, 27, 28, 31, 32, 39, 40, 47

cocoons 47, 48

common earthworm 17

D, E

daily cycle 28

earthworms 5, 6, 8, 11, 12, 14, 15, 16, 17, 18, 19, 20, 21, 22, 23, 24, 26, 27, 29, 31, 32, 33, 34, 37, 39, 40, 46, 47, 48

eggs 34, 47, 48

eyes 7, 12, 39

eyesight 7

F, G

feather-duster worms 10

feeding 12, 20, 21, 28, 30, 31, 39, 44

flatworms 5, 8, 9, 30, 34, 35

giant African worm 15

giant Australian earthworm 14, 15

giant forest-floor flatworm 30

gills 5

H, I

habitats 11

hair 12

head 35, 44, 47

hookworms 34

intestines 20

L, M

larvae 48

leeches 5, 44, 45, 48

length 12, 15

lugworms 5, 24, 25

mating 46, 47

mouth 16

P, R

predators 38, 40, 41

ragworms 12

resting 28

roundworms 5, 8, 34

S

saddle 16

sea mouse 12, 13

segments 16, 17, 44

senses 7, 39

skin 19, 39

sleeping 23

sperm 47

spines 12

spiral-gilled tube worm 10

suckers 34, 44

swimming 9, 44, 48

T, V, W

tail 16, 19, 35, 44, 47

tapeworms 12, 34

tentacles 12, 31

tube worms 5, 10

vinegar worms 12

worm casts 20, 24, 29, 32, 37

52